SHAWNEE CAPTIVE
The Story of Mary Draper Ingles

SHAWNEE CAPTIVE
The Story of Mary Draper Ingles

Mary R. Furbee

quarrier press

Charleston, WV

ISBN-13: 978-1-891852-29-9
ISBN-10: 1-891852-29-9

Library of Congress Number: 2000054883

Cover Design: Mark S. Phillips
Cover Illustration: L. Jason Queen

10 9 8 7 6 5 4 3 2

*This title was originally published in hardback by Morgan Reynolds, Inc.
under ISBN 1-883846-69-2, and is currently still available.*

Distributed by:

West Virginia Book Company
1125 Central Avenue
Charleston, WV 25301

www.wvbookco.com

For Jenny, my favorite daughter

Contents

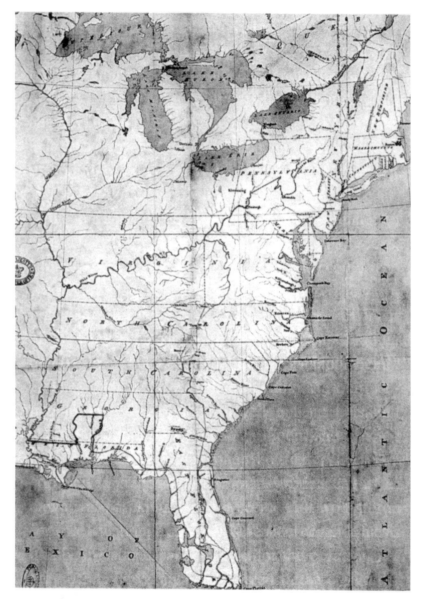

The American frontier that young Mary Draper and her family traversed in 1745 was a rugged and wild land.

Chapter One

The Journey

On a brisk summer day in 1745, thirteen-year-old Mary Draper and her family stepped onboard a ferryboat piloted by Evan Williams. The sky was as blue as flax flowers, and the sun shone brightly. Mary's chestnut brown hair escaped from her dusty cap as she shrugged her load onto the golden planks of the ferryboat deck. We might not have much, Mary thought to herself, but pickaxes, muskets, iron kettles, coverlets, and seed corn could surely wear a body down.

Evan Williams plunged his pole into the Potomac. As they started out across the river, he told the Drapers that his new ferry business was prospering. Since the previous summer when the treaty was signed with the Iroquois at Lancaster, travelers crossed the Potomac every day. Most passengers were Scotch-Irish like the Drapers, but English and German folks crossed, too.

The boatman talked of the German long-beards he had recently carried across the river. A strange lot they were, he said, walking single-file and clutching Bibles, without a woman among them. With all these immigrants, Evan Williams chuckled, the country was filling up as fast as a rat on a rafter.

As the ferryman chatted, Mary's father, George Draper, scratched his black beard and nodded. He was glad the Shenandoah Valley was opening up. He himself was headed to a job south of Staunton, building roads for Colonel James Patton.

George Draper and his wife, Eleanor, had been on the move for a long time. Ever since they left Ulster, Ireland, for America in 1729, they had been moving westward. Mary was born in Philadelphia in 1732, two years after her brother, John. But the affordable land was scarce near the city, so they headed west to Lancaster. With each move, the Drapers had tried to keep one step ahead of civilization and go where land was abundant and unclaimed. But their efforts were in vain. Only the very first settlers in an area could sink roots so deep that no man, army, or tribe could pull them up again.

Mary would never forget the summer of 1744, when Colonel James Patton first visited the Draper's cabin

Mary Draper and her family crossed the Potomac River on a ferry like this one on their journey to Lancaster.

near Lancaster, Pennsylvania. Patton had come to Lancaster to negotiate a treaty with the Iroquois Nation and to find buyers for western Virginia lands granted to him by the governor of Virginia. If the Iroquois gave up their claim to those same lands west of the Blue Ridge, Patton knew buyers would be plentiful.

It had been a big day when Patton and the delegation of men rode into Lancaster. People for miles around left their plows and spinning wheels to catch a glimpse of the negotiators. Governors, foreign ambassadors, land speculators—even a young journalist named Benjamin Franklin—came decked out in scarlet waistcoats, powdered wigs, and gold-trimmed hats. The delegates hailed from Virginia, Maryland, Pennsylvania, and the motherland, England, itself.

What a contrast there was between the elegantly dressed white delegates on horseback and the 200 Native Americans who straggled into town on foot. Mary thought most of the Native Americans seemed a sullen and threadbare lot in their skin shifts, loincloths, and second-hand white men's jackets. Only the chiefs dressed impressively. Copper beads hung from their necks. Hawk feathers and beaver fur crowned their black, glossy hair. Their soft skin clothing was embroidered with bright beadwork, porcupine quills, and bird wings. Mary stared hard at the chief whom settlers called Black Prince. Gunpowder tattoos crisscrossed his dark skin, and folks whispered that he must be half African.

Mary and her family joined other settlers who gathered to watch the Iroquois set up camp. While the women readied a meal over an open fire, Black Prince and the men smeared themselves with white paint and bear grease. Then they danced in a circle and chanted to beating drums. Mary's father said the Iroquois looked like the highland tribes of Scotland. Mary's mother said they looked more like the hounds of Hell than the saints of Heaven.

Madam Montour was a French woman who had been captured by the Iroquois as a child. As she walked through the Iroquois camp, the white spectators whispered and stared. Montour was of high birth, raised in a mansion with many servants to do her bidding. Yet she had grown used to Iroquois ways, married a chief, and had several children with him. It was rumored Madam Montour was a favorite among Philadelphia's Quaker ladies, who were friendly with Native Americans. These ladies invited Madam Montour to take tea with them in their homes.

By day, the Iroquois and white negotiators met in the courthouse. In the evening, the white hosts wined and dined the twenty-four chiefs on long, linen-covered tables. One hundred candles lit the room. The Drapers and their neighbors gathered outside, waiting to hear news of the proceedings. Mary and the other children stood on each other's shoulders and peered in the windows.

Two weeks after the negotiations began, the chiefs signed a treaty. They gave up ownership of their hunting grounds from the Blue Ridge to the Mississippi River. In exchange, the white delegates promised that the Iroquois would be able to hunt and travel in the area unmolested. The delegation also promised that the Valley's Indian Road would be improved and lengthened to make travel and trading easier. Most importantly, the English negotiators promised to form an alliance with the Iroquois against the French, who also claimed the area. A sack of gold coins, guns, and a few dozen mouth harps were thrown in to sweeten the pot.

After the treaty was signed, Mary watched one of the chiefs rise from the table. He called for wine to toast the alliance. The chief solemnly suggested to the waiters that they fetch English glasses, not French. After a startled pause, everyone broke into smiles and laughed. Then all lifted their glasses and shouted: "Long live the King of England!"

After the delegations departed, the town of Lancaster quieted while word of new land in western Virginia spread like wildfire from cabin to cabin. Less powerful tribes such as the Shawnee still claimed the Great Valley of Virginia and the Allegheny Mountains, but the treaty cracked open the door to settlement.

Through that crack, Colonel Patton aimed to bring as many of his Scotch-Irish brethren as possible. After the other delegates left Lancaster, Patton stayed and visited Scotch-Irish colonists living in and around the town. One of his first stops was the Drapers' cabin. The Drapers had once been neighbors of Patton's cousin and land partner, John Lewis.

When Patton came to call, Mary's parents gave him a warm welcome. The colonel drank ale, broke bread, and spun yarns about a great green glade surrounded on both sides by blue-shadowed peaks. He called it, "The Valley of Contentment and Strife." Mary and her brother hunkered down by the fireplace, drinking up every word that boomed from Patton's mouth.

Colonel Patton showed the Drapers his deed for a 100,000-acre tract of the Shenandoah Valley. The land stretched from the southern Shenandoah Valley to the New River, inside the western Allegheny Mountains. Patton told them that the Virginia governor gave him the land and granted permission for Scotch-Irish Presbyterians to settle and worship freely there. The story was different to the east, where only the state-sanctioned Church of England, or Anglican Church, was permitted. Patton had convinced Virginia officials that the fierce Scotch-Irish Presbyterians would not flee at the first sign of trouble from the French or Indians.

To Mary Draper, Colonel Patton seemed nearly as

awesome as the Presbyterian prophet John Knox himself. Patton had given up a rich business trading in indentured servants to carve out an empire from the wilderness. Patton had talked the Tidewater Virginia elite into allowing religious freedom.

As the colonel stood in the firelight of the Draper's cabin, he told them the future never looked so bright. Those willing to stand firm and work hard, Patton said, would do well to come and "grow up with the country."

Chapter Two

The Irish Tract

The Drapers and Colonel Patton shared a common—and bloody—history. During centuries of religious wars, Mary's lowland Scottish ancestors had wielded swords and pikes to defend Protestant monarchs fighting against Catholic armies. But the victorious Protestant kings and queens—firmly of the Church of England—were ungrateful. The English rulers had no tolerance for the Scot's Presbyterian beliefs, so they kicked them off their tenant farms in England.

During the sixteenth century, the English rulers resettled the Presbyterian Scots in the region of Ulster in the north of Ireland—on land stolen from native Irish Catholics. Bloody feuds erupted between the two displaced peoples. The English also passed laws discriminating against the Presbyterian Scots and charged them high rents. Worn out soil, crop failures, famine, disease—this was the lot of generations of Scotch-Irish, who also were called the Ulster Irish. As new-lyweds, George and Eleanor Draper, like hundreds of thousands of their countrymen, longed for a better life. In 1729, George and Eleanor sold what belongings they had and booked passage on a crowded sailing ship bound for the American colonies.

The Drapers headed to the colony of Pennsylvania, where all faiths were welcome. But in Lancaster, things turned out badly. The new immigrants settled on lands that Pennsylvania Quakers claimed belonged to the Native Americans. George Draper responded that was ridiculous. Heathen savages would only hunt on the land, but white men would bring forth the fruits of the earth as God had intended, George railed. The Drapers and their neighbors also resented how Americans already living in the New World boasted about their American ancestry. Mary's parents scoffed and called this false pride. A man who was prouder of his ancestors than of himself was like a potato—the best part of him was underground.

During their ten years in Lancaster, the Drapers tilled the soil and kept to themselves. Then Pennsylvania officials decreed that the Native Americans did not own the land after all—but neither did the Ulster Irish! Rich landowners from Philadelphia produced deeds for huge tracts of land, including the Drapers' farm. The Philadelphia landowners wanted the Ulster Irish to either leave, buy, or rent the land for high prices.

Mary's father raged that the Quaker governor of Pennsylvania, William Penn, had himself invited the Ulster Irish to come to Pennsylvania! They had come, marked their boundaries with tomahawks, and improved the land. They had transformed dense forest into valuable farmland. Mary's parents had enough of greedy landlords back in Ireland, so they pulled up stakes and headed to Patton's land in western Virginia. The new county, Augusta, stretched from the Blue Ridge Mountains to the Mississippi River. Amidst mountains that climbed to the heavens, only a few hundred white people lived. All who came got cheap, fertile land second to none in America.

Patton offered the Drapers land there for only four pounds and five shillings per hundred acres. When George Draper complained that he did not have the cash, Patton offered him a job building roads. Eyes gleaming, George Draper agreed on the spot.

The Drapers packed their gear, crossed the Potomac

on Evan Williams' ferry, and walked south to the Shenandoah Valley. For generations the Native Americans had burned the woods and brush to create pastureland that hugged creeks, rivers, and natural springs. Topsoil from the fires had rushed down a hundred streams and rivers into the now-rich glades and valleys. Buffalo, elk, deer, and other game that gathered at natural salt licks made easy targets. The animals' furs brought many shillings.

Under treetops so thick they hid the sun, the Drapers hiked along a narrow, overgrown trail carved by migrating buffalo, deer, and Native Americans. The Native Americans called it the Great Warrior Trail; settlers called it the Indian Road or Great Wagon Road.

George and John Draper hacked tangled grape and greenbrier vines from the path and felled trees to cross narrow creeks. At bigger streams the family waded right through, carrying their belongings on their heads to keep them dry. Near isolated cabins and small settlements, the trail widened to allow passage of small carts or wagons.

At Frederick Town, the first real village, the family stopped to rest. The trading post and inn run by a friendly German, Joshua Hite, were welcome sights. The innkeeper welcomed the Drapers with a hot meal and soft cornshuck mattresses. Unlike the German neighbors her family had feuded with back in Pennsylvania, Hite bursted with admiration for the Ulster Irish. Hite called Staunton, the seat of Augusta County, "the Irish Tract." He said it was home to good, hardy folk who prayed long, sang loud, worked hard, and drank hardily. The aristocracy might rule Philadelphia and Richmond, Hite boasted, but the backcountry belonged to the Ulster Irish.

The next 150 miles proved Hite right. Small Scotch-Irish settlements clustered along the Indian Road. The Drapers were offered so many mugs of cider, tea, and whiskey that it slowed them down. The settlers' children greeted Mary and John like long-lost cousins, luring them into the woods for a quick game of tag. Frisky as colts, the children leapt over brooks and tore around trees. Mary's parents tried to keep the visits short. They were eager to see their old Lancaster neighbors, John and Margaret Lewis, who had moved several years earlier to the Shenandoah Valley and founded Beverly's Mill Place.

Mary was excited to meet the Lewises, whom she had heard stories about since she was a toddler. John had fled Ireland after he killed an Irish landowner in a fight. Margaret Lewis had been wounded in the fray and still bore the scar on her arm.

At Beverly's Mill Place, the Lewises welcomed their old neighbors into their fine, two-story log house. After sharing news from Lancaster, Margaret Lewis showed Mary and Eleanor her "book of comfort." Margaret recorded every detail about her daily life in it. Margaret also showed them the wild roses she had dug from the meadows and planted around her front door. Then, over cups of raspberry leaf tea, Margaret told tales of their dozen years in the wilderness.

Her greatest trial occurred when a Native American boy kidnapped their daughter Alice. The boy had wanted to marry Alice, whom he called White Dove. John Lewis firmly refused. The boy and his friends grabbed Alice while she was berry picking. There was a skirmish between the settlers and the Native Americans. Eventually peace was restored when an old hermit, Mad Mary Greenlee, found Alice and brought her home. Alice had been a bit "teched in the head," Margaret told Mary and her mother. The child told crazy tales of being hidden in an underground palace with silver walls, pearl floors, and marble fountains. But Alice was a hardy girl and soon recovered her wits.

The Lewises were proud of their small town and took the Drapers on a tour. They stopped first at the whiskey still. No "revenuers" could tax his whiskey profits in Virginia as they had in Ireland, John Lewis boasted, as he handed around dippers full of the sourmash. The pale brew was strong enough to have a dead hog in it, John Draper later told Mary, but they drank it politely enough before strolling to the new log courthouse. After showing off the public whipping post, George and John Draper went inside the court-house with John Lewis. There John Lewis showed them great hand-drawn maps of the road George Draper was going to build. It would extend from Beverly's Mill Place to Patton's new settlement of Cherry Tree Bottom, on the silvery headwaters of the James River.

After resting a brief spell in Beverly's Mill Place, the Drapers continued their journey. The dirt road again became a narrow trail, and Mary's father viewed it with a keen eye. He would level and widen this path into a fine road. He would bypass this boulder, fell this ghostly sycamore, and bridge this brook with logs.

When the Drapers came to a 200-feet-deep gorge crossed by a natural stone bridge, they stopped dead in their tracks and gaped. George Draper said not even a granddaddy oak timber could have spanned this chasm, so God himself must have blessed his road-building project. Mary inched to the edge of the rock bridge and peered down carefully at the small creek below.

A couple of days later, the Drapers reached Robert Looney's Ferry on the upper James River. At the mouth of Purgatory Creek, a dozen log cabins nestled in a sunny clearing. Here, at the final stop on the Indian Road, Colonel Patton based his land surveying, developing, and selling operations. The Drapers found Patton in a small stone house, sitting behind a cluttered desk. Bonds, scales, and ledgers vied for space, as did books he brought all the way from Ireland: *Harvey's Mediations, An Account of Denmark,* and *The Dying Speeches of Convicts.* A huge sword hung on the wall behind the colonel's head.

Patton moved the Drapers into a vacant cabin in Cherry Tree Bottom, and George Draper began working on the road. Eleanor Draper readied up the cabin, and Mary and John planted small patches of corn and potatoes in black soil as soft as Irish moss.

Mary found that settlers in Cherry Tree Bottom were not much different from those in Lancaster. The Salleys, Renicks, and Millses helped each other at births, cabin raises, and harvests. They gathered for weddings and funerals. And, when they could spare the time for the journey, they attended church services at Tinkling Springs Presbyterian Church near Beverly's Mill Place.

Cherry Tree Bottom residents also were more tolerant of Native Americans than people in Lancaster had been, Mary discovered. Never before had Mary seen so many Native Americans. For weeks, none would appear. Then a dozen, or a hundred, Iroquois, Cherokee, or Catawba would arrive in town and camp for a night or two. Colonel Patton said to give them whatever they wanted, even when there was little to spare. Be friendly, Patton advised, but keep a rifle locked and loaded in case of trouble.

The first time the Native Americans came when the men were away, Mary and her mother were nervous. A small group of braves strode into the Draper's cabin and plopped down on the floor by the fire. Following Patton's advice, Eleanor handed them wooden trenchers piled high with cornpone and gravy, while Mary sidled over near the loaded rifle. When they had eaten their fill, they set the empty trenchers down and walked out as silently as they had come.

Mary learned that the Cherokee to the south had never claimed any of Augusta—and they cared too much about good trading with the settlers to make any trouble. The Iroquois and Shawnee behaved differently. Sometimes they stole chickens, or some foolish settler gave them whiskey and a fight broke out. Because the Native Americans outnumbered the settlers, Patton said the only way to deal with "ornery redskins" was to put up with their behavior.

Mary noticed that when Cherry Tree Bottom folks talked of skirmishes with Native Americans, they were divided over whom to blame. Once, a dozen Iroquois killed a man's hog because game was scarce. For revenge, the owner of the hog went to the Iroquois campsite with some friends. The settlers pretended to be friendly, drank whiskey with the Iroquois, and bid them goodnight. But the settlers hid in the woods until the Native Americans fell asleep, then they attacked. After the first gunshots the Iroquois jumped up, grabbed their loaded guns, and shot back. Eight settlers and four Iroquois died before both sides retreated.

The next Sabbath after the killings, Reverend Craig of Tinkling Springs Presbyterian Church railed against the settlers who had attacked the Iroquois. The reverend stood behind the pulpit with a glass of whiskey in one hand and a loaded musket in the other. Normally, Craig scolded those who spread grain to dry, swore on the Sabbath, or disobeyed their masters. But that day, the Glasgow-educated clergyman thundered at his flock that God did not condone murder—even of a Native American. The Iroquois had been peaceful, and the settlers had committed a cowardly act. Some Valley settlers agreed with Craig. But Colonel Patton was furious with the pastor. Although he had been named the chief lawman of Augusta County, Patton refused to arrest the men involved in the attack. They might have been foolish, but killing a Native American was not murder, Patton proclaimed.

The skirmish frightened some settlers so much that they moved back east of the Blue Ridge. That made Patton see red, too, because the frontiersmen had promised never to turn tail and run. Yet, most kept that promise and set about reinforcing their doors so bullets could not penetrate them. In Cherry Tree Bottom and neighboring villages, settlers built palisade fences around the biggest house. In times of trouble, everyone gathered together there until the coast was clear.

Chapter Three

A Home of Their Own

For the two years the Drapers lived in Cherry Tree Bottom, work filled Mary's days. She helped till the soil, shuck corn, and make soap with ashes and lye. She helped her mother spin flax, weave cloth, and cook meals in the big iron kettle that they brought from Pennsylvania. She tanned the hides of deer, squirrel, beaver, and raccoon that her father and John shot. Mary also tended the neighbor's sheep with John, keeping an eye out for ravenous wolves. Although they could have scared them away with gunfire, Mary and John killed all the wolves they could. The county paid a bounty for dead wolves because the predators preyed on the free-ranging livestock. Each wolf head and hide added coins to the family's savings, which they would use one day to buy land of their own.

So much work left little time for school. In Lancaster, Eleanor Draper had taught her children their letters using the Bible as their only text. On winter evenings in Cherry Tree Bottom, as tree limbs creaked and groaned in the howling wind, Mary and John continued their studies. By the light of bayberry bush candles and pine knot torches, they read Bible passages, copied psalms, and sang hymns. Mary was taught that God had cursed all humans to suffer the pains of this life. After death, they would enter either the fires of Hell or the joys of Heaven. Heaven would be their reward if they worked hard, sought guidance from the Bible, and obeyed their elders.

Mary mixed work and play when she could. While plucking feathers out of ganders with Colonel Patton's daughter Peggy, the girls would race to see who could clean the bird the fastest. Sometimes Mary went with John to fish in the James River for long-nosed, sharp-toothed garfish. Mary watched for fins breaking the surface as the crafty gar swam slowly through the shallows searching for crawdads. When Mary hooked a fish, it thrashed in the water trying to get free.

By the time Mary was fifteen, the Indian Road her father worked on extended to Cherry Tree Bottom. As soon as it was finished, wagon loads of new immigrants began pouring into the southern Shenandoah Valley. New mills, taverns, and trading posts formed the hubs of growing settlements. Wheat fields replaced patches of Native American corn. As trouble with the French simmered, the settlers built larger forts. Some forts had underground passages to springs, guardhouses, storehouses, and powder magazines.

Among the newcomers were many poor arrivals from the north of Ireland. George and Eleanor Draper, after years in America, could barely understand the thick brogue of their old homeland. Some of the immigrants purchased land, while others worked for several years as indentured servants in exchange for plots of land.

The immigrants' tales of suffering in Ireland brought back sad memories for George and Eleanor Draper. In Ulster, the new arrivals said, days had turned as dark as night, black frost had covered the rolling hills, and famine had set in. Homeless families roamed the towns begging for bread. Many were so desperate they abandoned their babies by the side of the road. Officials hired old women to collect the abandoned infants and take them to the workhouses. Once there, most of the babies died within days.

Such hardships bred hard men, and the hardest of the lot brought trouble to western Virginia. George Draper, who took an extra job as a county constable, found such men a sore trial. Mary's father hauled Patrick Save before the court for not bringing his children up in a Christian manner. He arrested Mary Wolfinger for stealing a horse and Matthew Young for beating Michael Bready with the butt end of his musket. One drunken trader, John Connally, was a horse-thief, gambler, and brawler. Mary's father said he was lower than a snake's belt.

Work as a constable brought in a welcome dollar. But George Draper was a man of the soil, as his family had been for generations. The Drapers longed to get their hands around the handles of a plow and turn over their own black soil. They wanted to hang a legal deed on the wall of a cabin that they built with their own hands. They wanted to grow a crop fine enough to take to market across the Blue Ridge—and to trade their profits for horses, oxen, hogs, sheep, a milk cow, and some waddling geese.

In 1747, their neighbor John Peter Salley visited the Drapers with news. He knew the family was scouting for land to buy and told them of a fine glade in the New River Valley, on the far reaches of Patton's grant. George trusted Salley's knowledge of the western lands, for he was one of the few white men who had set foot there. In 1742, Salley had floated down the

Mississippi on a raft made of buffalo hides. The French captured him near Natchez and made him a slave in their New Mexico mines. But Salley escaped and made his way home up the New River Valley. Salley told the Drapers that the New River area was rich with lead mines, salt works, buffalo, elk, and deer. Grass grew higher than a man's head, he said. Coal lay on top of the ground. The trees were so huge that one would provide enough wood to fuel a fire for years.

After George Draper visited the land that Salley described, he came back to tell his family he had found their new home. It was a paradise, he said, far from other settlers and miles off the Native American paths. The Drapers gave Patton their hoarded shillings in exchange for 500 acres, gathered up their gear, and trekked off into the mountains that rose into the sky like a string of beads laid on its side.

After climbing a high peak, the family stood on a plateau. Behind them, 1,000 feet below, the Shenandoah Valley stretched wide and green. In front of them to the west lay a forested, bowl-like valley, ten miles long and five miles wide. The Drapers descended the mountain until they found a grassy meadow by Strouble's Creek. There, a few miles from a horseshoe bend in the New River, they set up camp.

Mary's family built a small cabin in Draper's Meadow.

While George scouted for a cabin site and Eliza readied a meal, Mary and John gathered wood and water. Near the edge of the forest, a heap of fallen, charred logs caught Mary's eye. Next to it, a slick river stone stood on end in the ground. Mary knelt for a closer look. The epitaph scratched into the stone sent a chill down Mary's spine. "Mary Porter," read simple, childlike letters. "Killed by the Native Americans, Nov. 28, 1742."

The burned cabin and grave startled Mary and John, but their parents said it happened a long while back, and Indian troubles were passed now. Still, George and Eleanor warned Mary and John not to venture out of the clearing alone or unarmed.

Work helped chase away the children's fears. Together, the family built a twelve-foot-square, windowless log cabin, with one door and a small sleeping loft. Mary and Eleanor daubed mud from the bed of Strouble's Creek into the cracks between the logs.

After the cabin was up, Eleanor Draper nailed the deed for the land on one of its walls. George Draper strapped himself into a simple iron plow. John held the handles as George pulled, and the blade turned over the rich, black soil. When the ground was tilled, Eleanor and Mary helped plant their first crops of corn, beans, and potatoes. As Mary sowed seeds into the straight rows, her fears about lurking Native Americans faded.

Each day, Mary learned something new about the wild country around them. She discovered where to pick the fattest berries, which rock was the best for pounding clothes clean, and how far away a pack of wolves was by the sound of their howling. As the summer grew hotter, Mary and John slipped away into the forest to play. They climbed and swung on wild grapevines and creepers that hung from trees ten feet around. Where two creeks joined and tumbled over a mossy waterfall into a clear deep pool, they splashed, played, and washed.

The Drapers soon found themselves in the company of neighbors. A diverse group was drawn to the New River lands. Peggy Patton moved within visiting distance over on Reed Creek. The Germans Jacob, George, and Adam Harmon were crazy enough to live right on the main Native American trail. And the German long-beards, whom Evan Williams had ferried across the Potomac, built a tidy community on Dunkard's Bottom. Mary admired the religious men's neat houses and fields, but otherwise she thought they were odd. They had beards to their knees, lived without women, prayed for hours each day, ate no meat, and walked single file. If you asked a long-beard why he never married, he would reply: "He who marries did well, but he who did not marry did better."

Other newcomers bought land adjoining the Drapers', and soon a small settlement was born. The Leonards and Burks were of English stock. The Lybrooks hailed from Germany. And the Ingles family—widower Thomas Ingles and his three sons— were Scotch-Irish like the Drapers. The Ingles men built a gristmill that freed Mary and her mother from grinding their corn in a hollowed-out tree stump. The enterprising family also petitioned the House of Burgesses for a license to operate a ferry on the New River at Big Lick. But before permission was granted, the river flooded to the treetops. Mary was shocked when a traveler brought word that, back in Cherry Tree Bottom, the James River had washed away homes and crops. Residents carried their children to high ground through water up to their armpits or floated on roofs until they could grab hold of treetops. The Draper and Ingles families prayed for the souls of the dead and sent all the flour, corn, and meat they could spare over the mountains to the survivors.

For two years, life was good in Draper's Meadow. Their crops grew tall and hardy—and so did Mary. On the Sabbath, before sharing a midday meal, the Draper and Ingles families stood at their puncheon table and thanked God for their blessings. Mary enjoyed the company of her brother, John, and the three Ingles boys so much that she hardly ever missed the other girls she had known in Lancaster and Cherry Tree Bottom. On summer evenings, Mary ran as fleet-footed as the boys during games of fox-and-geese. Draper's Meadow folks laughed and called the lanky girl with the flyaway hair a wild colt, and wild colts, they all knew, made strong horses.

Mary had to be strong because life on the frontier was hard. Two years after the family arrived in Draper's

Meadow, tragedy struck. Mary's father, George, disappeared while out hunting. Men came from Reed's Creek, Dunkard's Bottom, Cherry Tree Bottom, and Beverly's Mill Place to search for him. They scoured the woods, but even the best trackers found no thread from his coat, no footprints in the mud, no blood on the ground. George Draper's trail just disappeared.

Mary and her family were left to worry and to wonder if he had been captured or killed by hostile Native American warriors, or eaten by a pack of wolves. Or had John Connally and his band of riffraff come over the mountain to take their revenge? Shortly before George's disappearance, the outlaws had ventured into the New River area and stolen livestock. Eleanor Draper had complained to Patton when the colonel had last stopped by while making a trip through his lands. The posse looked for Connally to question him, but he had fled to Cherokee country in the Carolinas.

Since there had been no warriors sighted in the area, George Draper was presumed dead. Mary and her family grieved, then faced the future. If Mary and John had been younger, Eleanor Draper might have sold her land and moved east, where life was easier. She might have bound herself and her children out as servants, or she might have remarried. But the Drapers were made of sturdier stuff. They decided to stay put and hold tight to their land. The Ingleses promised to help them, and the two families grew even closer, especially Mary Draper and Will Ingles.

A year later in 1750, New River Valley settlements buzzed with exciting news. An invitation had been issued far and wide to attend the first wedding between two white settlers in the area. Mary Draper, age seventeen, and Will Ingles, twenty, would be married at the Draper cabin. A traveling preacher would come on horseback to hear their vows, and a big celebration would follow.

When the wedding day arrived, Mary woke at dawn. John was already out of the house. Eleanor Draper had been up for hours, baking bread in the hearth ashes. On the fireplace spit, she turned a great hog that had been killed for the occasion. The previous fall, they had gathered goldenrod to dye Mary's new linsey-wool dress, so she could shine as bright as the sun. Red velvet ribbons bought from a passing peddler trimmed her long wavy hair and strong waist.

All morning, Mary helped her mother with the food, an apron across her gown to keep it fresh. At noon guests began to arrive. After a nod to the women, the men and boys went off toward the patch of woods between the Draper and Ingles' cabins. The women-folk visited and gossiped until they heard caterwauling loud enough to scare the devil.

Will Ingles had been riding to Mary's cabin in his new broadcloth suit. His brothers and father rode alongside. Suddenly, the male guests sprang from the woods and attacked them. Hooting and hollering, the men grabbed the wedding party off their horses and pretended to scalp them. When the party finally arrived at the Draper cabin, Will's new buckskin jacket was stained with mud and his bristly black hair stood straight on end like a Mohawk warrior's.

Mary laughed as Will slicked back his hair and straightened his jacket. Then the Harmons, Lybrooks, Ingleses, Drapers, and others, crowded into the tiny room. Mary stood by the fireplace, and Will joined her. Before God, preacher, and neighbors, Mary and Will vowed to protect and keep each other until death parted them. The gathered neighbors cheered. A gourd of fine mash whiskey passed from hand to hand. Then another cheer rose, as a young man in the back of the room cried, "Race for the bottle!"

Young men elbowed through the crowd and gathered in the dirt yard outside. Mary stood in the doorway of her family's cabin and yelled, "Ready, set, go!" The runners headed through the settlement, across a field of stumps, then disappeared into the woods. Several minutes passed. Finally, the wedding guests heard a distant hoot. At that owl-like call, Will Ingles held up a jug of moonshine wrapped in a festive spray of ribbons. Another man fired a musket into the air.

As the smoke rose, distant caterwauls filled the air. The hoots and hollers grew louder as the young men sprang from the woods. They leapt over stumps, brooks, stones—racing for the bottle as fast as they could. The winner grabbed the bottle as others straggled in, gasping for breath. Everyone cheered and struck the winner on the back as he carried the bottle to Mary, bidding her to drink. Then he called, "Let the dancing begin!"

The wedding guests pushed the cabin's few furnishings to the wall. A fiddler played jigs and reels, and couples old and young took the floor. The dancing lasted until dawn, and anyone who tried to sleep in a corner was grabbed up and made to dance. Just as dawn was breaking, when it seemed all would drop from exhaustion, a raucous serenade began. Guests grabbed pots and pans brought for the occasion. As they banged away, young women in the crowd descended on Mary.

The rabble-rousing drummers were shooed outside. The women stripped Mary of her wedding dress and slipped on her bedgown. They tucked her into the new cornshuck mattress in the loft and pulled a new woolen coverlet over her. Giggling, the women then ducked outside. The young men in the crowd grabbed Will, pushed him in, and shut the cabin door. Outside, all joined in the cheering and dancing in the light of a brand-new day.

Mary and Will were wed in Draper's Meadow.

Chapter Four

War Comes to Draper's Meadow

Mary and Will tilled their fields and took their crops to market. With their earnings, they bought a horse for riding and a pair of oxen for plowing. In five years, they had two sons, whom they named after the boys' grandfathers: Thomas and George. Eleanor Draper lived with the young couple and helped raise their children. Mary's brother, John, married pretty Bettie Johnson from back in the Valley. Soon she was like a sister to Mary.

George Draper had been right. The New River land was rich with opportunity. Mary and Will cut down more forests and tilled more fields. They grew wheat for market, flax for cloth, hemp for rope, and rye for whiskey. Will even started to talk about hiring on some indentured servants to help in the fields.

One July, when her babies were infants, Mary

stepped out of her cabin and greeted a strange procession led by the strapping Colonel Patton and a Cherokee chief called Little Carpenter. The colonel was escorting a delegation of Cherokee from the Carolinas to Williamsburg, the capital of Virginia. There they would debate over trade and alliances.

Mary offered the group refreshments and smiled politely. But secretly she worried. The need for negotiations meant that the troubles with the French were threatening to boil over. Around the world, the French and British empires were fighting. Now that fight was coming home to the American colonies. Patton had been courting the Native Americans' favor for more than a decade, but so had the French. So far, the Cherokee sided with the English, but the Iroquois were wavering. And the fierce Ohio Shawnee were already mixing war paint and sharpening their tomahawks to aid the French.

Mary was right about the brewing conflict. From 1752 to 1755, New River Valley settlers began to have trouble with Native Americans. Colonel Patton advised them to keep the peace if at all possible and to fight only if attacked. Most followed his advice. When a group of Cherokee stole Adam Harmon's entire stock of furs, he remained calm and decided to follow

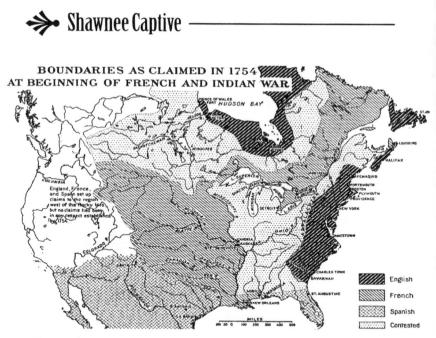

BOUNDARIES AS CLAIMED IN 1754
AT BEGINNING OF FRENCH AND INDIAN WAR

English
French
Spanish
Contested

This map shows how America was divided at the beginning of the French and Indian War.

the law. He rode over the mountains to Beverly's Mill Place and got a warrant for the Cherokees' arrest. But other settlers were hotheaded and craved revenge. After another rash of thefts, the bodies of three murdered Cherokee were found by the New River.

A handful of settlers were worried enough to return east. After Alexander Max's cornfields were burned, he dreamed that a raiding party descended on the area, burning cabins, scalping settlers, and taking captives. Alexander packed up, headed for civilization and urged others to follow. Mary and Will stayed put, determined to protect what they had worked so hard to build. Yet they also pleaded with Colonel Patton to send soldiers to patrol the frontier.

Will wrote Patton a letter, warning that if the Native Americans and French drove people off the frontier, eastern Virginia would face the scalping knife next. Patton showed Will's letter to Virginia's leaders in Williamsburg, but the plea fell on deaf ears. Virginia's leaders were busy gathering an army under General Braddock to march through Pennsylvania and take Fort Duquesne from the French. Colonial officials said frontier folks had to protect themselves, for soldiers could not be spared.

In July of 1755, however, Patton finally got permission to muster a small patrol for the New River area. On July 6, the colonel and the soldiers arrived. That same day, the French and Native Americans slaughtered Braddock's troops to the north, fueling a war that would not end until 1763. The French and Indian

British General Edward Braddock led the attack on Fort Duquesne against the French.

War, fought between the English, French, and Native Americans, stained the frontier soil red with blood. During the continued fighting over land in the American colonies, the war spread to Europe, where it was known as The Seven Years' War.

Draper's Meadow settlers and Patton's brigade of a dozen militiamen were unaware of Braddock's defeat and the full-fledged frontier warfare it unleashed. Unbeknown to them, the woods now crawled with bands of French-allied Native Americans on the warpath. Colonel Patton sent his soldiers to scope out the area. He remained in a cabin he kept in the Meadow to do some paperwork on land sales. The farmers of Draper's Meadow made plans to harvest their wheat, for times would be lean if the golden grain went to ruin.

The next morning, Colonel Patton sent his nephew William Preston to Sinking Creek to fetch Philip Lybrook to help with the harvest. Will Ingles, John Draper, and a few other men and women headed through the woods to their bottom fields. The men carried scythes over their shoulders. The women carried hemp ropes to bind the wheat into bundles for threshing. In their fields, they sliced, raked, and bundled the ripe stalks in the hot sun. Mary was pregnant with her third child, and Bettie was nursing her new baby girl. They stayed behind to fix a big midday meal for those working.

Morning passed. Eleanor watched the boys play in the clearing. Mary cooked by the hearth, and Bettie harvested garden vegetables for the stew pot. Bettie's baby slept peacefully in a hollowed-log cradle. All was peaceful. No one suspected that a dozen war-painted, French-allied, Shawnee warriors were creeping quietly toward the clearing, their tomahawks raised.

Mary knew that the Shawnee fought because the settlers were moving onto their land, turning it into farmland and driving away the game. But Mary believed Native Americans were heathen savages who wasted the land by not cultivating it. Taming the wilderness, being fruitful and multiplying, tilling the earth—Mary believed that was God's work. Anyone who stood in the way of that deserved defeat.

The Shawnee crept toward Draper's Meadow thirsty for revenge. They sought revenge for stolen lands and lost game; revenge for their fallen braves at Fort Duquesne; and revenge against Patton, the lawman of Augusta who had not arrested the Cherry Tree Bottom murderers years before. Here, in these mountains, the Shawnee drew the line. With help from the French, the English conquest of their homeland would be stopped.

When Mary heard Bettie's piercing scream, she knew with a jolt of fear that the enemy was upon them. Throwing down her spoon, she ran to the door, looking frantically about for her boys, her mother, Bettie, and Colonel Patton.

But it was too late. A warrior with a single feather in his jet-black hair held Mary's sobbing sons by the scruffs of their necks. Another stood over her mother's lifeless body, waving a scalp of long, gray hair above his head. Bettie, running into the forest with her baby in her arms, was shot as Mary watched. The bullet hit Bettie's arm, and her baby fell to the ground. With her good arm, Bettie picked up her daughter and kept running. But a warrior caught her and grabbed the baby. Mary watched in agony as the shooter dashed the baby against the cabin wall. Bettie howled and collapsed on the ground.

Mary ran toward her boys. The brave holding the boys pushed Mary to her knees. Her arms twined tightly around weeping Georgie, age two, and Thomas, age four. Across the settlement, Mary watched as three warriors burst in upon Colonel Patton. The old colonel howled in anger and grabbed his broadsword. Before he was shot dead, Patton sliced into two braves, killing one and wounding the other. Mary feared that at any moment she and her boys would meet the same fate as Eleanor and Colonel Patton.

The Shawnee ransacked the cabins for everything of value. Mary watched them bring out her mother's old black kettle and the guns and ammunition that Patton had brought from the east. Strapping the loot onto the settlers' horses, two braves paused to slash open Eleanor's feather beds. The braves laughed as clouds of white feathers billowed through the air.

The chief, with a shaved head and massive chest, stopped the laughter with a sweep of his arm and a stern command. He pointed to the cabins and barked out an order. Hastily, the others gathered Mary, her two boys, and Bettie into a huddle and set the settlement on fire with the embers of Mary's own cooking fire.

The Shawnee motioned to their captives to rise quickly. They feared pursuit, Mary realized, as she was hefted onto the only horse not loaded with stolen goods. In that moment, Mary realized that Will and John would have heard the gunshot and smelled the smoke. They would send someone to investigate.

The braves lifted Georgie in front of Mary and Thomas behind. The threesome clutched each other tightly. Mary worried about poor Bettie, who fared much worse. Forced to walk, she stumbled along blindly, weeping and clutching her bleeding arm. God shaped his children's backs for their burdens, Eleanor Draper had always said. But Mary thought poor Bettie's burden the heaviest of all.

The party headed toward the woods leading to Strouble's Creek. But before reaching the treeline, two keen-eyed braves bringing up the rear suddenly stopped. They pointed back at the settlement and yelled. The warriors had spotted Will crouching in the woods watching the party leave. Will had told the others to hide while he went to check on those back in the settlement. Now, as the two braves ran toward him, he leapt to his feet and ran through the forest.

The main party of Shawnee entered the forest at a brisk pace. They headed down the mountain toward the New River. Mary stared ahead of her and prayed that Will would get away. When the two braves returned without a scalp, she was sure that he had outwitted them somehow. Mary's relief that Will was alive mingled with her grief over her mother's death, her worry about Bettie, and her fear for her children. It would take Will and John a couple of days, she thought, to round up Patton's militiamen for a rescue party. But Mary could not guess at what Will would soon find out: The Shawnee had ambushed and killed

Mary Draper Ingles, Bettie Draper, and their children were taken captive by the Shawnee.

the soldiers, just hours before the attack on Draper's Meadow.

All her life, Mary had heard about Native American captives who were killed to exact revenge, sold as slaves, or adopted. Only a handful of settler families were able to ransom or rescue their loved ones. When the braves riding ahead of her turned to look behind them, Mary tried to read their painted faces. They looked severe, she thought, but less bloodthirsty than in the clearing. Mary prayed that the killing was over.

After a few more miles the party stopped at a clearing, and two braves dragged Casper Barber from his cabin. Mary covered her boys' eyes and turned away her face as the braves cut off Barber's grizzled white head. They put his head in a cloth bag and continued down the path. Next, they would pass Philip Lybrook's place. Mary longed to cry out an alarm to his wife and children, but fear that her own children would be killed before her eyes silenced her.

At the Lybrook's, Mary watched a single brave leave the group and walk calmly to the cabin door. Mrs. Lybrook answered the door, then shrank away. But the brave held up his palm as a sign of friendly greeting. He smiled and handed her the bloody sack with Casper Barber's head in it. Then the warrior turned and rejoined the party. Shortly afterwards, the group stopped at the creek and washed the paint off their faces. With Barber's death, they had avenged the death of the man Colonel Patton had killed with his sword.

Mary found the strength to soothe her children, who had begun whimpering when Casper was killed. But even as Mary's mind worked, her body began to fail. The weight of her swollen belly bouncing on the saddleless horse felt like it would break her back. She thanked the Lord for the support of her small sons' bodies in front of and behind her.

Mary stared at the swaying rump of the horse ahead of her. On each rump were two painted hand prints, one red and one blue. Mary's worries about Bettie continued. She knew that Native Americans killed captives who slowed their progress, and Bettie could barely keep up. She stumbled along the rough path—barefoot, unseeing, and weeping. With her good arm, she clutched her shattered one. Mary longed to call a word of comfort, but did not dare. When Bettie fell and moaned, Mary pled silently for her to get up and keep moving. Mary's eyes swung to her captors' faces, watching for signs of anger as Bettie rose.

As the day faded into dusk, gnats hovered about the captive's sweat-covered faces. Hunger burned like hot coals in the pits of their stomachs. The horse's sweaty withers rubbed the insides of Mary's legs raw. She felt as if the kicking baby would soon drag her to the center of the earth. Mary's hope for rescue faded as she realized a horrible truth: The men of Draper's Meadow were outnumbered, and the Shawnee had guns and powder.

When at last the group halted, Mary almost cried aloud with relief. The chief hauled Mary off the horse. On his dark cheeks, two parallel red lines ran from the corner of each eye to his jaw. Between the stripes were three blue dots. A single eagle feather rose from a silver medallion attached to the back of his head, and heavy silver pieces rested in his long, drooping earlobes. The chief motioned to where the captives should gather and sleep. After relieving themselves as best they could, they obeyed. Because they had no blankets, they huddled together for warmth and slept.

The next morning, the party traveled for two hours before eating a scant breakfast of ground corn mixed with spring water. Mary's boys ate greedily. That afternoon, the chief gestured for Mary to fix food for everyone. Mary made Johnnycakes on the rocks by the fire. She handed the browned, steaming corncakes to her captors first. She thought the chief looked almost pleased. This gave her courage to try to get water to bathe Bettie's wound and poor blistered feet. All the captives were barefoot, for they rarely wore shoes in the summer. But only Bettie had been forced to walk the entire journey over the deadfalls, twigs, and briers that littered the damp forest floor.

Mary kept her face as unreadable as her captors'. She walked over to one of the horses and tore a piece off her petticoat. She dampened the cloth from the dangling leather water bag. Then, with her head high and her huge stomach jutting out before her, Mary walked to Bettie's side. She dabbed the dried blood and pus from Bettie's arm. When Bettie gasped and whispered that the chief was coming, Mary stared straight ahead.

Mary knew that her life might well be finished, but she could not let Bettie die of infection. As the chief's dark brown hand extended toward her, Mary shrank away. But his hand, she soon saw, did not hold a tomahawk or knife. Instead, the chief offered a bundle of healing comfrey leaves. Startled, Mary watched as he crouched down beside her. He demonstrated how to bundle the leaves and place them on the wound, under the cloth bandage. Mary nodded and did as he had shown.

The chief's actions proved to Mary that the Shawnee wanted them alive and well, at least for now. Armed with this new knowledge, she took heart. After bandaging Bettie's arm, Mary walked again to the horses. She rearranged the looted goods packed on the horses so Bettie could ride. Mary helped Bettie mount, then sat little Georgie up in front of her. The men made no move to stop them. A warrior helped Mary and Thomas onto their own mount as usual.

As the group moved on, Mary kept an eye on their route. Although their captors were tolerating them now, terrible trials could lie ahead. They could be killed, tortured, adopted, or sold into slavery. If the chance came, Mary thought, they should escape and make their way back to Draper's Meadow. To do that, she would have to remember the trails and know how to escape this fearsome wilderness that few settlers had ever seen before.

Near dusk on the second day of travel, the group came to a hunting shack where Indian Creek dumped into the New River. While some of the party swam the horses across, others hauled two leaf and rock-filled canoes out of the water. The elm bark boats were laced together with grapevines and braced with branches. To Mary they looked half-rotten from being hidden on the riverbed. But the canoe held fast as the men, using stiff sections of oak bark, paddled the captives and stolen goods across. On the other side, the Shawnee seemed less afraid of pursuit. They camped earlier in the evening and rested longer. They nodded in a friendly fashion when Mary brought them their dinner and even smiled at the boys.

Mary did not know what to make of this. If their captors liked the boys, would they be treated better? If so, that was good. But what if her children were drawn to heathen ways? As her boys experimented with Shawnee words and watched the braves with keen interest, Mary shivered. She prayed that Will and a rescue party were close behind. But in her heart she knew that chances grew slimmer with every passing hour.

Every hour also brought Mary closer to having a child that might share the fate of Bettie's baby. So far, the Shawnee had treated her and her sons better than she could have hoped. But if they thought the infant would slow them down, Mary did not doubt that its tiny skull would be crushed in an instant. On their third day in the wilderness, her baby dropped low in her womb. Cramps wracked Mary's body. Her water broke and drenched the horse beneath her. She held tight to Thomas so that she would stay on the horse. She resisted asking that the party stop.

But Mary's worst fears were never realized. The way she had stood up for her family, helped others, and submitted to orders had greatly impressed her captors. Now she was in labor, on a horse, without uttering a scream or cry. Her captors felt this woman with the wide brown eyes and firm mouth was as strong as most Shawnee squaws. She would make a fine Shawnee, much valued by whoever adopted her to replace a sister or mother, dead from a massacre or disease.

It was late afternoon by the time Mary could no longer take the pain. She tried to dismount from her horse, and when she hit the ground her legs buckled beneath her. Thomas quickly scrambled off the horse and helped his mother up. Mary told him to stay with the others. She headed into the woods bent over at the waist.

The chief motioned for the party to stop and set up camp. He gestured for Bettie to follow Mary. That night, Mary's boys slept by the warriors' side as she gave birth through gritted teeth. She did not cry out as she had with the first two. She understood that fortitude was a captive's salvation. When her tiny daughter with a full head of jet-black hair emerged, Bettie cleaned the newborn with a piece of her petticoat. With another scrap, she swaddled the baby and laid her in Mary's arms. Mary and the baby slept. Bettie, grieving for her own lost baby, kept watch through the night.

The next morning, the men were absorbed in a game with Mary's sons. They had fashioned a target from a strip of green hickory for the boys to practice their aim. While her sons were throwing makeshift spears, Mary emerged from the woods with Bettie and the infant. The boys dropped their game and ran to their mother and new sister.

Bettie held Mary upright. She sent the boys for a dipper of water, and Mary drank. While the Shawnee captors watched expressionlessly, Bettie and the boys helped Mary mount her horse. Bettie placed the swaddled babe in Mary's arms. Thomas scrambled up behind to support his mother's back. It was only the fourth morning of their captivity, but to Mary, it felt like a lifetime.

Chapter Five

Bound for Ohio

As Mary's pain subsided, she began to pay attention again to their route. Sometimes the party followed the tumbling New River. But they also veered off onto narrow overland trails that crisscrossed the mountains. Mary soon gave up trying to memorize the twisting paths. If we ever escape, she thought, we will have to follow the river home.

The party stopped at a salt spring for a few days to make salt. Deer and elk antlers littered the shoreline, because the animals came here to lick salt and shed their horns. Thomas and Georgie soon forgot that they were captives and ran about gathering as many sun-bleached horns as they could find.

Mary and Bettie were put to work boiling saltwater in the kettle that came from Mary's own hearth. When all the water evaporated, the valuable salt was left in the bottom. The men killed a deer, and the roasted and salted meat eased the captives' hunger. Mary searched the woods for berries, roots, and more comfrey leaves for Bettie's arm. Escape crossed Mary's mind as she foraged alone. She was tempted, for only God knew what fate awaited her. But her infant and boys were alive and well. Bettie's arm was stiff but not infected. Mary knew she could not leave her children and Bettie behind.

The group made as much salt as they could carry. Then they followed the river through an area of meadows and cane fields. Sometimes the trail followed the river; other times it veered off into the forest. Mary felt sure they still followed the New River, but the men called it the *Ka-na-wha*. A few days later, the Kanawha dumped into a body of blue-green water, three times wider than any Mary had ever seen. Mary heard the men say *O-yo-o*, or Ohio. She knew they had reached the river that John Peter Salley had ventured down in his bark boat.

The party camped for a night on a spit of land where the Kanawha River dumped into the Ohio. The next morning, they walked to a swampy area buzzing with mosquitoes. Again the men brought forth hidden canoes, and the group crossed the Kanawha. From there, they continued down the eastern bank of the Ohio through rich bottomlands and brush-free stands of trees. Clouds of birds dove across the water at dusk. The party traveled along the Ohio for several days, first south, then west, following the river's course. In other hidden canoes or on foot they forded tributaries that dumped into the great river.

One day, a change came over the warriors that worried the captives. Mary and her family were removed from the horses and told to walk. Then the warriors stopped and donned the war paint that they had been wearing on the day they attacked Draper's Meadow. That afternoon, Mary was startled when they arrived at a cornfield. She wondered if there could possibly be a settlement this far west, and if the warriors were about to attack it. Then Mary saw a dome-shaped hut covered with slabs of elm bark. An old man with a face like cracked leather walked through the animal skin door. He greeted the men with a raised hand, then sent two young boys in a canoe to the western bank. Soon, several long, sturdy-looking canoes, paddled by young teenage boys, surged across the great river. The returning warriors loaded the stolen goods and captives into the boats, and the boys ferried them swiftly across the wide water.

The canoes turned up the shaded Scioto River. Neat fields of corn, peas, and tobacco and hundreds of huts like the old man's lined the riverbank. The huts clustered about long, low-roofed lodges five times as big as Tinkling Springs Church. As they glided up the creek, a mob of men, women, children, and wolf-like dogs ran alongside the bank. As the dogs barked and howled, the crowd pointed at the canoes, shouting and laughing.

The canoes pulled up at a long, open yard in the center of the village. The yard of the Lower Shawnee Town swarmed with villagers. Mary's courage left her as she was pulled from the canoe. The Shawnee brandished weapons, wailed war cries, and waved Colonel Patton's and Eleanor Draper's scalps in the air. Mary's boys cringed against their mother in fear. Rough hands grabbed Mary, Bettie, and the boys. They were pushed toward the crowd, which parted to make a path into the village common. The captives clung to each other as the villagers pinched, slapped, spit, and hissed at them. Mary ordered her boys not to cry and to keep moving.

The Shawnee tied the captives to red and black painted poles in the center of the village. The returning braves talked with a broad-shouldered older man in an

otter skin turban. Then the warriors and other men of the village went into the council house for a feast and dancing.

A half-dozen settlers already sat tied on nearby poles. Mary looked over the bedraggled captives. Her glance stopped at a proud-looking old woman with wild gray hair. Although they might all be burned at the stake at any moment, the woman wore a broad, toothless grin. In broken English, she told Mary that her name was Mrs. Stump. Her group had been captured in Pennsylvania after the French and Native Americans had defeated Braddock at Fort Duquesne. They had arrived at the town the day before and had not eaten since, Mrs. Stump said. The old woman said she did not know what the Shawnee were going to do, but it looked like they would have to run the gauntlet.

Mary looked up and saw that Mrs. Stump was right. From the tales of former captives, Mary and Mrs. Stump knew a little bit about the horrible ordeal that lay ahead. A double line of Shawnee children, old men, and women had formed. It looked as if they were about to dance the Virginia Reel, but their angry fists clutched sticks and bramble switches. Mary and Mrs. Stump coached the captives to rush between the lines and keep their heads covered as their captors beat them. Do not stop no matter what, they said. If you make it to the end, you win their respect and live. If you fail, you die.

Bettie was among the first dragged to the two lines of shrieking villagers. Gripping her bad arm, she ran forward as heavy blows rained down on her legs and back. Bloody and bruised, she made it to the ninety-foot longhouse at the end. Mrs. Stump made it too. Although Mrs. Stump was more than twice Mary's age, she was a big, broad woman with large muscles. Mary cheered Mrs. Stump as she charged as fiercely as a bull.

When she saw that others had endured the torture and passed the awful test, Mary took heart. She girded herself for her turn, but because she had won the warriors' admiration on the trail, she was spared the ordeal of the gauntlet.

Later the next day, the captives were led into a longhouse where the villagers and members of neighboring tribes had gathered in a great circle. The returning warriors stood in the circle and told the stories of their successful raids. Mary and the other captives did not understand the strange-sounding words. But the men's facial expressions, movements, and pantomimes made common language unnecessary. Braves stepped in the circle and acted out the killing of Bettie's baby, Colonel Patton, Mary's mother, and Casper Barber.

The one who pointed to Bettie fell to the ground and clutched his arm. He pretended to cry and he screamed. Then he showed how Bettie had helped Mary with the birth of her daughter. When he finished, an older man walked into the circle, took Bettie's arm and led her away. Bettie and Mary locked eyes, and Mary pled silently with her sister-in-law and friend not to give up hope.

One by one, other warriors stepped into the council circle to imitate a captive. Mrs. Stump, Mary saw, was admired. The man who told of her capture stood with his hands on his hips wearing a sassy grin, and the audience roared with laughter. Mrs. Stump grinned as she was mocked. Mary, too, admired her courage.

One by one, men claimed Mrs. Stump and the other captives. Finally, Mary stood alone holding her infant with her boys clutching at her skirts. Then the chief of the raiding party stepped forward. The handsome warrior pointed to the boys, smiling and gesturing, and Mary knew what was coming. She might never see her sons again. They would soon forget their mother, father, and newborn sister. Mary held the boys tightly and whispered to them to be good. She promised that their father would come for them soon. She told them never, ever to forget her and to say their prayers each night.

Two men emerged from the circle and dragged the crying, struggling boys away. Mary could not stop her tears. The men were from other villages. They left the longhouse, loaded the boys on horses, and rode off in separate directions. Mary had hoped that the boys would be adopted together and stay where she could see them. But the Shawnee often separated family members so they would sooner forget their birth families and grow attached to their new Native American ones. Mary felt that her heart would break. She waited for someone to take her daughter and then herself.

Now the chief acted out how Mary had cooked for the braves and dressed Bettie's wound. He told how she had repacked the horses, quieted her children, and given birth without complaint. The audience laughed as the chief puffed out his stomach to imitate a pregnant woman—grunting and screwing his face up tight as he pretended to give birth.

Mary felt sick. She did not want the admiration of the men who had murdered her mother and stolen her sons and best friend. She only wanted the ordeal to be over. But what happened next stunned her. After the chief finished talking, a young woman led both Mary and her baby to a vacant hut. She was given a blanket and food and left alone with her child.

The ordeal was over, and Mary still had her baby girl. Because she did not speak the Shawnee language, Mary could not understand what had happened. Two days passed. Mary's relief slowly turned to dread. The captives who remained in town walked about as if they did not care if they lived or died, and Mary almost envied them. Unlike the other captives, Mary still had something very precious to lose: her last child. Worry clawed at her insides.

Mary wondered why if she were admired so much some important chief had not adopted or married her. Then she learned the answer. Two French fur traders, who operated a trading post in the village, had made a deal with the Shawnee. The Frenchmen took Mary to their hut. With gestures and broken English they explained that the Shawnee were allowing her to work for them. The traders said they would pay her for making the long calico shirts that the Shawnee loved. A Shawnee wet nurse would care for her baby while she worked.

Mary grabbed at the chance. It meant keeping her daughter with her and no adoption or marriage, at least not yet. Eleanor Draper had taught her daughter to sew a neat stitch, and Mary's deft hand created flawless shirts for the traders. She imagined that she might be able to earn enough money to buy her children's freedom.

Mary's sewing pleased the Frenchmen and their customers. Her first knee-length men's shirt created quite a stir. The brave who bought it paraded around the village for all to come admire. Soon, there was a waiting list for Mary's shirts. By day, she worked hard, hoarded her coins, and kept her face shut tight as a mussel shell. At night, she held her daughter close, missed her family, and ached to be free.

September arrived, and the nights cooled. Maple, oak, and hickory leaves began to turn yellow and red. Mary had learned a few Shawnee words. Huts were called *we-gi-wa*. *Ta-ku-wha* was bread. *Nee-gah* was mother. But Mary rarely used these words. Taking advantage of her status as seamstress for the French, she kept to herself. Still, she could not help watching the adopted captives in the village. Those who cried, cringed, or refused to learn Shawnee ways were mocked and given difficult jobs. Those who adapted were treated with respect and affection. Mary thought of Bettie and hoped she was faring well.

Mary also watched captive children. Most of them, she noticed, adapted quickly. This did not surprise Mary, for a child's memory is short and the Shawnee treated captive children like blood kin. At least her boys would be loved, but they would soon forget their Christian teaching. Then Mary saw young boys playing at scalping with small tomahawks. She winced and turned away, unable to bear that her sons might grow up to hate, and even kill, their own people.

In early October, the Frenchmen told Mary to get ready for a salt-making expedition to Big Lick Salt Springs. Mrs. Stump was going too, and Mary was glad for the company of another white woman.

A dozen warriors, the Frenchmen, a few squaws, and the two captives formed the party. They set off down the Ohio River in a flotilla of canoes. About 150 miles down river, the canoes turned up Big Bone Creek. Three miles up the creek, they pulled up onto a grassy shoreline. The area once had been a swamp. Ancient mammoths, buffalo, saber tooth tigers, and other beasts had wandered into the muck, gotten stuck, and died. Their bones had surfaced and now jutted from the ground. The sun had bleached the bones white, and the rain had washed them smooth. The Shawnee erected rough shelters by piling saplings against twelve-foot-long mammoth tusks they had found sticking out of the creek bank.

Among the great bones, Mary and Mrs. Stump boiled brine and cooked the company's meals. The Shawnee and Frenchmen did not fear the women's escape so far out in the wild and set the women to work foraging for berries, wild grapes, and edible roots. Mary and Mrs. Stump were each given a tomahawk for digging and cutting and a wool blanket, which they tied around their shoulders for warmth. Mary's new freedom gave her courage. Others had surrounded and watched her back in the village. But here, while a loving woman tended her baby, she roamed freely.

Mary had mourned her mother, missed Will, and worried about her children and Bettie for too long. Any day, the Frenchmen might move on to another village. Then the tribe would treat Mary like the other captives. She would have to give up her only remaining child. She would have to marry a Shawnee, even though she was married to Will already and doing so would be a sin against God.

These thoughts gave Mary new determination. She had to escape while she had the chance. Three months had passed since the raid on Draper's Meadow. Mary could no longer survive on a dim hope of rescue. She

had to try to get home to Will and John. She had to tell them that their children and Bettie were alive and awaiting help.

Chapter Six

Escape Through the Wilderness

Mary and gray-haired Mrs. Stump grew to be close friends at Big Lick Salt Springs. Mrs. Stump told Mary of her childhood in Germany, and Mary told her about Draper's Meadow. Mary found the older woman's courage and good humor comforting. Mary told Mrs. Stump she planned to escape and asked her to come with her. At first, Mrs. Stump was horrified. The Native Americans will chase, kill, and eat us, she said. Draper's Meadow is hundreds of miles away, and we would get lost. Winter is coming and we would starve. Worst of all, the baby girl surely would not survive the trip. Mary was crazy, she said. It was impossible.

But Mary knew they could make it. She told Mrs. Stump that the Shawnee would think they had gotten lost in the wilderness. The first leg of the journey is back up the Ohio, she reasoned. If we get caught, we can claim we got lost. We will steal a little corn before leaving, and then steal more when we pass the Shawnee fields on the way upriver. All we have to do, Mary said, is follow the rivers.

Explaining to Mrs. Stump that she would leave her baby behind, and why, was much harder for Mary. It tore her heart out to leave the infant, but she knew the nursemaid would protect the child until Will could rescue her. Finally Mary's arguments won Mrs. Stump over. For several days they hoarded parched corn, but not much, because they did not want anyone to notice. Then, one day while out gathering food, they walked north along the Ohio River without looking back.

Mary had no idea how hard the journey would be. She and Mrs. Stump would pass through the wildest country east of the Mississippi. Traveling on horseback and in canoes with the Shawnee was a far cry from traveling alone on foot. Herds of buffalo and elk had worn solid paths along the Ohio. But many wide rivers poured into the Ohio, blocking their way. Neither woman could swim, and the Shawnee hid their canoes well. They had to hike up the tributaries until the water was shallow enough to wade across.

There were no paths along most of the tributaries they encountered. Mary and Mrs. Stump hacked through tangled vines, brambles, and laurel with their tomahawks. Finally, when the rivers were only waist high, they inched their way across the slippery stone riverbeds. Chilled to the bone, they hiked in sopping skirts and drenched moccasins.

For the first few days, the weather held, and their clothes dried before the chilly nights fell. When darkness came, they wrapped up in their blankets and burrowed inside piles of leaves. They snuggled close for added warmth. Knowing they had each other meant the world to both women, and they encouraged each other as best they could.

After a few days, they had eaten all of the stolen corn. Foraging only netted a few dried grapes and nuts, and Mrs. Stump's good humor disappeared as quickly as the corn had. She grumbled nonstop about her empty belly. Mary realized that this woman who had handled the trials of captivity so well could barely abide the pains of hunger.

Mary and Mrs. Stump hiked on and on. On good days, they found paw paw trees laden with sweet yellow fruit, stands of red tea-berries, and crisp Jerusalem artichoke tubers that tasted like turnips. Then Mrs. Stump was like a child on Christmas morning. On bad days, when they found nothing, Mary's companion sank into despair. Again and again, Mary told Mrs. Stump not to give up. She promised they would find food when they reached the old Shawnee homestead across the river from the village. And, finally, they did. Two weeks after they had set out from the Big Lick Salt Spring, the village of their captivity appeared across the river. Mary and Mrs. Stump quickly backed away from the path and into the forest to avoid being seen. In the woods, they crept toward the old man's homestead that Mary had first encountered months before.

At the edge of the clearing, they stopped and crouched low. No one walked about and no chickens pecked in the dirt yard. No smoke rose from the hut. The homestead seemed deserted, but Mary insisted on waiting until dusk. When the sun had gone down, the women approached and peeked inside the hut. There was no fire pit, blankets, baskets, weapons, or food. The old man had abandoned his *we-gi-wa*. It was risky, but the women longed to have a roof over their heads again. So Mary and Mrs. Stump made the hut theirs for a night. They went inside, wrapped themselves in their blankets, and collapsed.

Just before dawn, Mary awoke with a start. Her heart pounded loud and fast. A horse snorted outside and from his neck a bell clanked softly. The old man has returned, she thought, and he is outside.

Mary woke Mrs. Stump and reminded her that if they got caught, they would say they had been lost in the woods. They crept to a crack in the bark wall and looked out. In the yard, a lone horse grazed lazily. Around its neck hung a bell on a leather strap. Otherwise, the yard was empty. Mary and Mrs. Stump stared wide-eyed at each other as they realized their good fortune.

Quickly, they caught and tethered the horse. They gathered stray kernels and ears of corn from the field, which they wrapped in a blanket and tied to the horse's back. Mary took the bell off the horse's neck to throw it away, but Mrs. Stump insisted on keeping it. They stuffed the bell with leaves and grass to keep it from clanging. Then they hurried up the Ohio. Only when safely away did they stop to eat. They pounded the kernels of white corn on rocks with the backs of their tomahawks and stuffed the powder into their mouths, washing it down with water from the river. For the first time in days, Mrs. Stump smiled.

The two women took turns riding the horse, and the pains in their feet subsided. On the gentle, old mare, Mary was more hopeful than she had been in days. But after three days of hiking up the Big Sandy River, seeking a place shallow enough to cross, discouragement again set in. In desperation, Mary and Mrs. Stump finally decided to try crossing at a logjam from a recent flood. Sticks, trees, and brush had formed a bridge across the water. The pile of debris looked deep and strong, but there was no way to be sure. Mary tugged the reluctant horse, and the old woman pushed. At the center of the river, the horse's legs suddenly rammed through the brush and into the swirling water below. Tangled in the mesh of logs, the old mare neighed and tossed about trying to get free. The women tried desperately to pull the animal loose as the logjam creaked and threatened to break apart. Mary and Mrs. Stump had no choice but to scramble ashore and leave the poor creature behind. The horse's cries followed them as they walked back down the other side toward the Ohio.

After several days, the women had eaten the last of the corn. Deer, elk, pheasants, and flocks of wild turkeys, fattened up for their winter's rest, clattered away through the forest as they approached. Muskrats, minks, raccoons, beavers, and frogs dove into the water to escape them as they passed. But Mary and Mrs. Stump had no gun, bow, or trapping skills. A few slow frogs were the only animals they managed to catch. They devoured these raw in seconds. Foraging for plants also turned up only a few berries and nuts, and again Mrs. Stump began to mutter. In desperation, the women began pulling up unknown bushes and gnawing on their roots. Some of the roots were crisp, white, and filling—like turnips. Others were woody and sour and brought on fits of dizziness, nausea, and vomiting.

Mary had not remembered so many tributaries blocking the path up the Ohio. Some were shallow enough to cross on foot, and a couple of times the women found hidden canoes to use. But often they had to hike for hours or days up a tributary before they could cross and come back down the other bank. Mary's vision began to blur, and she had to stop for long rests until it cleared.

By late October, Mary and Mrs. Stump had been walking for three weeks. One night as they slept, an early winter snow blanketed the earth. With no other choice, they rose the next morning, dusted themselves off, and walked on. Mary told her hungry, scowling companion they had only two options: We walk, or we die. Later that day, they came across a deer head thrown away by Native American hunters. The hungry companions tore into the rotten flesh.

Mary and Mrs. Stump used hidden Shawnee canoes to cross rivers.

Mary had almost given up hope when they arrived at the Kanawha River. Her heart lifted as she recognized the spot as the place her Shawnee captors had found the hidden canoes and crossed to where they now stood. Mary stood at the mouth of the river, thinking, while Mrs. Stump sulked several feet away.

Mary decided not to search for canoes or to try to cross the river. On the other side was the maze of well-worn trails she had traveled during her forced journey. She knew she would never find her way on the twisted paths and worried that they might also encounter Native Americans.

Finally, Mary made up her mind. She told Mrs. Stump they were halfway home. We just hike up this western shore of the New River, she said. And then we will be home. Mrs. Stump only stared at Mary with glassy eyes. Mary patted the old woman gently, then turned and limped up the west bank of the New River with Mrs. Stump shuffling behind.

Mary and Mrs. Stump may have been the first settlers to walk through the razorback ridges of the New River Valley. They scrambled up cliffs, hiked on ledges, and crawled through laurel brakes. They tripped over forest debris that had been washed off the steep slopes during storms. Their makeshift moccasins soon fell apart. Black-and-blue bruises and blood-encrusted scrapes and wounds disfigured their swollen feet. Briers and brambles tore their dresses to shreds.

The two women passed the site where Daniel Boone would build his cabin twenty years later. They passed the sites of later frontier forts where the female scout Anne Bailey served thirty years later. They passed a curious pool of water called Burning Spring that sent up a stream of natural gas. Many decades later it would give birth to a flourishing new industry. Near Paint Creek, Mary and Mrs. Stump passed ancient stone walls built long ago by Stone Age people.

Mary and Mrs. Stump passed the Kanawha Falls on their difficult journey.

The river twisted this way and that. Mary attempted to save miles of walking by taking overland shortcuts. They crawled up steep slopes. Then to save wear on their aching feet, slid back down on their bottoms. By November, the birds and other creatures had eaten most of the fallen fruits, nuts, and berries. The women's hunger was so great that they tore into the soft inner fiber of tree bark.

At the wide Falls of the Kanawha, they passed the mouth of the Gauley and headed up the New River. Mary kept an eye out for the spot on the opposite bank where four months earlier the captives had stopped to make salt. Again and again, rock outcroppings robbed the river of a shoreline. Later settlers named these landmarks Penitentiary Rocks, Blue Hole, Pope's Nose, Lover's Leap, Hawk's Nest, War Ridge, Fire Creek, Castle Rock, Stretcher's Neck, and Big Flattop Mountain. But Mary gave them no names. She just climbed, crawled, and pulled her way up and down, over and around. Above her, ridges jutted thousands of feet in the sky. Below her, the river was a tumbling froth of churning white foam.

During their days of backbreaking strain, the women ate little. Mrs. Stump grew more and more difficult. She grabbed roots from Mary's hands. She screamed at Mary for having talked her into escaping. Again and again, Mary soothed and calmed her. She sang her lullabies, rubbed her feet, gave her larger shares of whatever they found to eat. When that no longer worked, Mary tried to keep some distance between them.

Just when Mary felt unable to walk another step, they came to the spot where her captors had left the New River and taken a trail through the woods. Only days remained in their journey, if they could survive.

Chapter Seven

Home at Last

Only days from home, the women's progress slowed. They stopped often to rest. They had eaten little more than a few hickory nuts, stringy bark, and sour roots. After crossing Scarey Creek, dusk began to fall. Mary began looking for a protected place to sleep, while Mrs. Stump rooted about for something, anything more to eat. In desperation, she pulled a bush up by its roots and threw it to the ground. Then a wild look came into Mrs. Stump's eyes. She trudged toward Mary, brandishing her tomahawk in the air and screaming she would eat "May-re Ink-les." Mary backed up and spoke soothing words to the old woman. She offered to give Mrs. Stump money when they got home. She offered to draw straws to see who should live and who should die. But Mrs. Stump let out a low growl that grew louder and louder before she charged.

Mary was young, but bone-thin and weak. Mrs. Stump was old, but she was large and stronger. When she got close, Mary grabbed her upraised arm, and they fell together, rolling and panting on the hard ground. The struggle was short, for both were too feeble to fight. For a few moments, the exhausted women clutched each other on the ground, gasping for air. Mrs. Stump began to regain her strength first and reached again for the tomahawk. Quickly, Mary summoned her remaining strength and pushed her away. Scrambling to her feet, Mary fled as fast as her emaciated body would carry her up the New River. The older woman sat on the ground, gasping for breath.

Upriver, Mary slipped under a riverbank and hid. As darkness began to fall, Mrs. Stump passed by. She muttered to herself in German and called out for Mary in English. By the time her voice faded away, it was dark. The moon rose high in the night sky, and Mary continued along the riverbank alone. Providence was with her, for she discovered a submerged canoe in the weeds. Thanking God that the river was low and the current was calm, Mary emptied the boat and shoved across. Mary only had a stick for a makeshift paddle.

At first the boat angled back and forth like a water bug, but Mary finally made it across.

Mary had more luck on the opposite shore. A short way up the river, she found an abandoned hunting shack. Surely she was nearing civilization at last, she thought. She entered the shack and collapsed on an old cornshuck mattress that felt as soft and wonderful as her mother's old feather bed. In the morning, Mary found two small turnips where a vegetable patch had been. She ate them raw and thought it the best meal of her life.

As Mary continued her journey up the river, she heard a familiar voice calling her from the opposite shore. Mrs. Stump stood on the opposite shore, fell to her knees, and begged for forgiveness. She pleaded with Mary to return to her side of the river. Mary had come to love the old woman. She knew the hunger and fatigue had driven her mad, but she feared that the madness might still be upon her. Mary hollered back for Mrs. Stump to keep going and not give up hope. We are almost home, she cried.

But Mary still had thirty miles to travel, and it was the end of November. She could no longer feel her feet. Much of the time her vision blurred. Yet Mary could smell, taste, and see her home. She smelled woodsmoke and felt Will's strong arms holding her tight. She dragged one foot in front of the other. When her strength faltered, she crawled on all fours like a wounded forest animal.

On the second day after Mary left the hut, the river shoreline suddenly disappeared. In its place was a 300-foot overhanging cliff that later settlers called Anvil Rock. The rock face had no ledges, shelving rocks, or footholds to climb on. The mountain around it was a straight wall of fallen rock, saplings, and loose soil. Mary fell to the ground and hid her face in her hands. She cried, she screamed, she prayed to God to deliver her. Finally, her fury and grief spent, she rose painfully to her feet.

First Mary waded into the river and tried to climb around the base of the cliff. But the ledge soon dropped off into a deep, bottomless pool. Frozen to the bone, Mary scrambled back to the bank and fell unconscious.

The next morning, Mary woke knowing that she was near death, but she was determined to keep moving until the end. Mary shrugged off her damp blanket and turned slowly onto her back. She let the November sun seep through the tattered clothing that clung to her brittle bones. An hour later, she stood and faced the sheer mountainside between herself and her home.

Her arms hung by her side like thin branches. Her eyes were huge in her shrunken face. Her raven hair had turned as white as snow. Slowly, Mary put one foot in front of the other. Painstakingly, pausing often, she climbed. Saplings and shrubs were the rungs of the ladder that Mary used to pull herself higher and higher. The climb took her nearly all day, and it was the most terrible day of her life.

When Mary reached the summit, she fell into a faint. When she woke, the sky was tinged with red. Draper's Meadow was only a few miles away. Mary rolled, slid, and scooted down the other side. She landed on her stomach, caught her breath, and shook her head to clear her vision. Before her, she saw a miracle: a cornfield and a hunting shack made of saplings and bark. Mary dragged her bruised and scratched body through the corn. As she crawled, she cried out hoarsely: "Help! Help!" Within minutes, three men came toward her slowly with rifles raised.

Adam Harmon and his sons had been camping at their hunting cabin. They were preparing to leave because of Native American alarms in the area when they heard Mary's weak cry and went to investigate. At first, the old, half-naked woman crawling on all fours made them suspicious. Native Americans sometimes used white captives to lure their enemies into ambushes. Fearing a trick, they held back. But when Mary drew closer and cried again, Adam Harmon gasped. Surely, that must be Mrs. Ingles' voice, he said. Then the grizzled old hunter ran forward to help his friend and neighbor.

When Adam Harmon carried Mary into the cabin, her bones felt as thin and brittle as kindling wood. Adam and his sons laid her on a pallet and wrapped her in blankets. They heaped wood on the fire and killed a calf to make some healing beef soup. Mary had used up every ounce of her strength getting home. Now she was like a newborn infant, unable to talk or feed herself. Adam Harmon and his sons held her up and fed her spoonfuls of beef broth. The men soaked and bathed her swollen bloody and frostbitten feet and legs. It was two days before Mary could talk again.

When Mary began to regain her strength, she told them she had escaped from the Shawnee village along the Ohio River and traveled through 800 miles of wilderness to get home. She said she had started out with a German friend. Then she shook uncontrollably as she related how the old woman had lost her wits and tried to kill and eat her. The tale brought tough old Adam Harmon to tears, and he was shocked when

Mary asked him to go find Mrs. Stump. Horrified by what Mary had told them, the Harmons refused to go. Mary lacked the strength to argue. She asked about Will and John. Were they both safe? How long would it take to get to Draper's Meadow? What the Harmons told Mary shook her further.

After the raid, Mary's and Bettie's husbands had joined with a few local men and followed the raiders. But they lost the trail and returned home. Then they begged Virginia officials to recruit militiamen to go after the Shawnee in Native American Territory. But raids were so common that militiamen had to stay and protect the local population. Forts sprang up all over the Shenandoah Valley and the New River territory, including one at nearby Dunkard's Bottom.

But Will and John had refused to give up. As Mary had hoped, they attempted to ransom their families. The brothers-in-law had gone with the scout Christopher Gist to friendly Cherokee country in the Carolinas. They would ask the Cherokee, then at peace with the Shawnee, to offer a ransom for Mary, Bettie, and the children. The men had been gone now for several weeks.

Mary's heart swelled with love for her husband and brother. Like her, they had not given up on reuniting their family. But fear also consumed Mary. She could not bear it if she had come all this way only to lose the remaining members of her family. Her husband and brother had been gone so long, and Mary feared the worst.

Mary was still weak a few days later. She started at every hoot of an owl or tree cracking in the forest. The Harmons told her that raids had led dozens of settlers to gather ten miles away in the fort at Dunkard's Bottom. After only a few days of rest, Mary begged the Harmons to take her to the fort at once.

At the fort, astonished settlers flocked around Mary. The women hugged her fragile bones and cried. They dressed her in clean homespun clothes and brushed out her long, matted hair. Everyone was anxious to learn her story. Many found it almost too incredible to believe that Mary Draper Ingles had walked through 800 miles of wilderness in forty-two days.

Mary again begged Adam Harmon and the other men at the fort to go after the "poor old woman." Mary pleaded that without Mrs. Stump she would have died. Starvation had addled the German woman's wits, she said, and she had no control over what she had done. The men succumbed to Mary's pleas and set off down the New River. Fifteen miles later, they heard the clanking of a horse bell and a faint voice crying, "Halloo!"

The old woman had found her own hunting shack on the other side of the river. When she arrived, it looked as if the hunters had run away in a hurry, for a still-warm kettle of meat sat on the fire. Clothes hung on the wall pegs. Most blessed of all, a horse grazed outside. The old woman had devoured every bite of meat—and every other morsel of food in the place. Then she dressed in leather britches and a buckskin jacket. Around the horse's neck she placed her lucky bell, now un-muffled. Mounted, she headed up the river toward Mary Ingles' home. "Halloo!" she cried every few moments in case anyone was near. When the men from Dunkard's Bottom found her, Mrs. Stump asked if dear Mary Ingles had sent them. When the men said yes, she grinned from ear to ear.

When Mrs. Stump tottered into the fort on her bare, purple feet, an angry silence fell on the room full of Mary's friends. Slowly, Mary rose from her rocking chair by the fire. Tears filled her eyes. She opened her arms, and the older woman ran into them. For a long moment, the two women wept, and the people in the room joined them.

Will Ingles and John Draper were camped only

seven miles away when the Harmons brought Mary to Dunkard's Bottom. Through Tennessee and Georgia they had visited Cherokee villages asking for help in finding and ransoming their families. The Shawnee had taken hundreds of captives, the Cherokee said. They would not give any up, especially during wartime.

Filled with despair, Will and John headed home to wait for spring, when they would try again. But their grim faces turned to joy when they rode into the fort and heard the news. Mary was inside, and their family members were alive. Will wept to see Mary and to hear that Bettie and the children still lived. The men watched Mary's haunted eyes and listened to her story of suffering. She left a young, vibrant woman, twenty-three years old. She returned a walking ghost.

That winter, Mrs. Stump returned to her home in Pennsylvania, and Will tried to nurse his wife back to health. But it was as if Mary had used up all her courage. She suffered fully from all her losses. Mary slept fitfully, lived in terror of Native American attacks, and sank into deep melancholy moods. Will moved Mary to Vause's Fort, twenty miles east at the head of the Roanoke River. But Mary's fears only grew worse. So they traveled through the Great Valley and over the Blue Ridge. In Bedford, far from trouble, Mary began to heal. Will knew that he had done the right thing. Soon after they left Vause's Fort, the Shawnee attacked it. One of his brothers died in the fight.

With Mary safe in Bedford, Will joined a militia unit and a band of 130 friendly Cherokees on another rescue mission. The Sandy Creek Voyage aimed to find and return Shawnee prisoners to their families. Mary and Will were bitterly disappointed when the campaign failed and they grieved over what Will had learned: Shortly after being adopted, Georgie had died. There was no word of four-year-old Thomas Ingles, the baby girl, and Bettie Draper.

Will told Mary that during the negotiations, the Shawnees learned for the first time that Mary and her friend had escaped. The astounded Shawnee had thought the women were lost in the wild. Both became legendary for making it through parts of the New River Valley that even the Native Americans had not penetrated.

Despite the dangers, Will Ingles wanted to return to the mountains. Without the farm, he told Mary, they had no wealth, no independence, no life. If everyone flees, he said, the Native Americans and French will win. If settlers do not defend the backcountry, they will soon be here in Bedford. Mary was deaf to his pleas that she return, and several years passed before she agreed to leave the safety of Bedford.

Each spring, Mary bid Will goodbye as he rode to Draper's Meadow. Late each fall, she welcomed him back to Bedford again. Most years, he returned to find a new baby in the house. Mary bore five more children—two sons and three daughters. She kept John, Mary, Susan, and Rhoda close by her side, and they brought her comfort. But their presence did not fill the deep hole left by losing Thomas, Georgie, her baby girl, and her best friend, Bettie. During all those years, Mary and Will never gave up trying to find their family. Will joined several expeditions into Shawnee country across the Ohio. But each time his attempts at ransom or rescue failed.

In 1762, Mary agreed to go back home. The Ingleses had sold Draper's Meadow and bought land several miles away on the New River. With every harvest, Will added to the family's land holdings. He built a larger log cabin and started a ferry across the New River. The new poled ferry brought in three pence for every man, horse, or cow that crossed. Next to the ferry, he built an inn and tavern.

In the coming years, Ingles Ferry became a prosperous frontier settlement. The family owned several thousand acres. They hired a few indentured servants to work in the fields and tavern. The sturdy log house had reinforced doors and a sleeping loft big enough to double as a fort when hostile Native Americans were near. A strong palisade fence surrounded the house. Will and Mary called their home Fort Hope.

In 1763, the French and Indian War finally ended, and John Draper finally won Bettie's release. Bettie told her family that a kind old man in a village on the Chillicothe River had adopted her. Bettie replaced his daughter who died and was treated with great affection. Despite that affection, Bettie could not shake her longing for her home and husband. She escaped once but was recaptured. The tribe sentenced Bettie to be burned at the stake, but Bettie's Shawnee father hid her. Then he talked tribal elders into changing their minds. After that, Bettie determined to adjust so that she could survive. Her nursing skills earned her a reputation as a medicine woman, and the village treated her with respect.

Bettie told Mary and Will that Thomas was well and living with the Shawnee in a village near Detroit. Will offered a handsome reward to hunters for the return of his son. But it took five more years before he succeeded in his efforts to bring Thomas home.

One spring day in 1768, Will Ingles returned to Fort Hope from another journey to look for Thomas. As usual, Mary came to the door to welcome him and hear his news. But she had long since stopped expecting to see her son with him. At first, Mary wondered who the young Native American man was riding on a second horse. Then she noticed the young man had brown hair, not black, and that his eyes were hazel. Mary's hand went to her mouth, and she began to tremble. Oh Will, she thought, you have brought my Thomas home at last. She forced her legs to move and went forward to greet her long lost son.

Afterword

In 1763, the French and Indian War ended, but Native American troubles continued through the Revolution and beyond. Ingles Ferry withstood Native American attacks three times. Mary's log house protected her family and her neighbors well.

The Ingles' tavern, farm, and ferry prospered. Will built a large, comfortable house overlooking the river. The two-story log home had two big rooms downstairs and two upstairs, an outside kitchen, and glass windows. Mary still worked at her chores every day, but she never regained her old strength. As they grew older, her daughters helped her manage the household.

In 1774, Will and Thomas Ingles—who gradually readjusted to white ways—joined an expedition against the Shawnee. With an army of Virginia Regulars and militiamen, they marched to a spot Mary knew well:

the point where the Kanawha meets the Ohio. There they fought against 1,000 Shawnee braves in the Battle of Point Pleasant. The royal governor of Virginia, Lord Dunmore, did not arrive to help the western Virginians fight the Shawnee, as he had promised. Then the governor signed a peace treaty with the Shawnee instead of pursing them into Ohio. Will and Thomas came home and told other settlers of the royal governor's betrayal. Tensions between Virginia's royal governor and western Virginians escalated.

After the Battle of Point Pleasant, Thomas returned to Augusta County and married. He and his bride moved to the fringes of the frontier. Four years later, Native Americans attacked. While Thomas worked in the fields, his wife and children were captured. Thomas pursued them, and in the fight that followed, warriors killed his two children. Thomas rescued his wife, but she had been tomahawked. A surgeon removed thirteen pieces of skull fragments from her head, and she survived.

Mary and Will, like most western Virginians, sided with the Patriots in the Revolution. In 1776, Will joined the Patriot Committee of Safety for Westmoreland and Fincastle counties. In 1777, he took an oath of allegiance to the Patriot cause, and he served as a colonel in the local militia. The militia mostly fought off more Native American raids—this time by Native Americans who sided with the British.

During the Revolution, Will suffered from bouts of illness. In 1782, at fifty-three-years-old, he traveled to the County Court in Staunton and declared himself unfit to serve. In September, he died at home. Shortly after that, Mary moved from the big house to the first house Will had built at Ingles Ferry. Mary's grown children asked why she would move back to the simple, one-room cabin with no widows and a dirt floor. Mary answered that it was further from the road and the river, and she felt safer there.

Mary Ingles lived in her cabin for thirty more years. In 1815, she died at age eighty-three, surrounded by loving children and grandchildren. The cabin of Mary Ingles stood for a long time. But rain, wind, and snow took their toll. The roof caved in, the walls crumbled. Finally, nothing stood but the chimney. Many years later, proud descendants of Mary Draper Ingles tore down the chimney and carted the rocks to Mary's grave. There they built a monument to their foremother, one of the bravest women who ever lived on the American frontier.

Research and Sources

———•◆•———

Mary Draper Ingles' son John was born eleven years after Mary returned home. After his mother died, John wrote down the story of her captivity and escape. Other friends and relatives wrote down what they recalled of Mary's story, too.

Over the years, several historians have pieced together those accounts and other information about the Native American wars in western Virginia in the 1700s. John P. Hale, who wrote *Trans Allegheny Pioneers* in 1931, researched comprehensively before publishing his account of Mary's captivity and escape. Such research made it possible for me to write this book.

This book tells the true story of Mary Draper Ingles' captivity and long journey. Yet competing versions of Mary's story exist. For example, different accounts of

Mary's story offer different dates. Some say the Drapers moved to the New River Valley in 1747; others cite 1753. Mrs. Stump's name is also a bit of a mystery. She might have been Mrs. Stumf—or had another name entirely. John Ingles did not mention the baby of Mary Ingles in his account of his mother's captivity and escape. However, other friends and descendants did write about the baby. It seems likely that Mary's son did not want it known that his mother left a child behind of her own free will. He probably thought people would not understand.

Recommended Reading

Founding Mothers: Women of America in the Revolutionary Era. Houghton Mifflin, 1975.

Fritz, Jean. *Can't You Make Them Behave, King George?* Paperstar, 1996.

Fritz, Jean. *The Double Life of Pocahontas.* Putnam, 1983.

Furbee, Mary Rodd. *Outrageous Women of Colonial America.* John Wiley & Sons, 2001.

———. *Women of the American Revolution.* San Diego, CA: Lucent Books, 1999.

Hakim, Joy. *From Colonies to Country* and *Making Thirteen Colonies* (History of U.S., Books 1 & 2). Oxford Univ. Press, Inc., 1998.

Kamensky, Jane. *The Colonial Mosaic: American Women 1600-1760* (Young Oxford History of Women in the United States, Vol. 2.) Oxford Univ. Press, 1995.

Moody, James, *Myths of the Cherokee.* Publisher: New York, Johnson Reprint Corp. [1970]

Bibliography

Atkin, Edmond. *Indians of the Southern Colonial Frontier, The Appalachian Indian Frontier; the Edmond Atkin Report and Plan of 1755*, edited with an introd. by Wilbur R. Jacobs., Lincoln: Univ. of NE Press, 1967.

Atkinson, George W. *History of Kanawha County*. Charleston: *WV Journal*, 1876.

Bailyn, Bernard. *The Peopling of British North America: An Introduction*, New York: Alfred A. Knopf, 1986.

Billings, Warren M. *The Old Dominion in the Seventeenth Century; A Documentary History of Virginia: 1607-1687*. Chapel Hill: Univ. of NC Press, 1975.

Blackwood, James R. *Tinkling Spring, Headwaters of Freedom: Protestantism and Liberty*. The Presbyterian Church in the United States, 1950.

Brooks, Geraldine, *Dames and Daughters of Colonial Days*. Salem: N. H. Ayer Co., 1984.

Cartmell, Thomas Kemp. *Shenandoah Valley Pioneers and Their Descendants*. Winchester, VA: Eddy Press Corp., 1909.

Conners, John A. *Shenandoah National Park: An Interpretive Guide*. Blacksburg, VA: McDonald & Woodward Pub. Co., 1988.

Cook, Roy Bird. "The Annals of Fort Lee." Charleston: *West Virginia Review*, 1935.

Craighead, James Geddes. *Scotch and Irish Seeds in American Soil: The Early History of the Scotch and Irish Churches, and Their Relations to the Presbyterian Church of America.* Philadelphia: Presbyterian Board of Publication, 1878.

De Hass, Wills. *History of the Early Settlement and Indian Wars of West Virginia*, Philadelphia: Wheeling, H. Hoblitzell, 1851.

DeNoya, Mary Musselwhite. "Massacre at the Meadows." *Daughters of the American Revolution Magazine,* 106(2): 132-136, 230, 1972.

Dexter, Elisabeth Anthony. *Colonial Women of Affairs.* Clifton, NJ: Augustus M. Kelley, 1972.

Dickson, R. J. *Ulster Immigration to Colonial America, 1718-1775,* Belfast: Ulster Historical Foundation, 1976.

Dodderidge, Joseph. *Notes on the Settlements and Indian Wars.* McClain Printing Company, 1824.

Ebersole, Gary L. *Captured by Texts: Puritan to Postmodern Images of Indian Captivity.* Charlottesville: Univ. Press of VA, 1995.

Egloff, Keith and Deborah Woodward. *First People, The Early Indians of Virginia.* Richmond, VA: The Virginia Department of Historic Resources, 1992.

Ellet, Elizabeth. *The Pioneer Women of the West.* Philadelphia: Henry T. Coates & Co., 1873.

Elstain, Jean Bethke. *Public Man, Private Woman: Women in Social and Political Thought.* Princeton Univ. Press, 1981.

Etienne, Mona, and Eleanor Leacock. *The American Revolution: Changing Perspectives.* ed. William M. Fowler, Jr., and Wallace Coyle, Boston: Northeastern Univ. Press, 1979.

Evans, Sara M. *Born for Liberty: A History of Women in America*. New York: Macmillan/The Free Press, 1989.

Fischer, David Hackett. *Albion's Seed: Four British Folkways in America*, New York: Oxford Univ. Press, 1989.

Frost, John. *Pioneer Mothers of the West; or, Daring and Heroic Deeds of American Women*. Boston: Lee and Shepard, 1859.

Garland, Robert. *The Scotch-Irish: A Social History*. Chapel Hill: Univ. of NC Press, 1962.

Green, Harry Clinton and Mary Wolcott Green. *The Pioneer Mothers of America: A Record of the More Notable Women of the Early Days of the Country, and Particularly of the Colonial and Revolutionary Periods*. New York: Putnam's and Sons, 1912.

Hale, John P. *Trans-Allegheny Pioneers*. Cincinnati: The Graphic Press, 1886.

———. *History of the Great Kanawha Valley*. Madison, WI: Brant, Fuller and Co., 1891.

Hale, John S. *A Historical Atlas of Colonial Virginia*. Staunton, VA: Old Dominion Publications, 1978.

Hall, Grace M. "Under the Cover of Darkness," *West Virginia Review*, June 1942, 155.

Heatwole, Henry. *Guide to Shenandoah National Park and Skyline Drive*. Luray, VA: Shenandoah Natural History Association, 1995.

Hennepin, Louis. *Women and Religion in America, Vol. 2,* ed. Rosemary Radford Reuther and Rosemary Skinner Keller, San Francisco: Harper and Row, 1983.

Howe, Henry. *Historical Collections of Ohio*. Cincinnati: C. J. Krehbiel and Company, 1902.

Howison, Robert Reid. *A History of Virginia from its Discovery and Settlement by Europeans to the Present Time.* Philadelphia: Carey and Hart, 1846-48.

Hyde, Arnot. *Pictoral History of the New River: A Photographic Essay,* Charleston, WV: Cannon Graphics, 1991.

Ingles, Andrew Lewis, ed. *Escape From Indian Captivity,* Radford, VA: Commonwealth Press Inc., 1969.

Jennings, Francis. *The Ambiguous Iroquois Empire: The Covenant Chain Confederation of Indian Tribes with English Colonies from Its Beginnings to the Lancaster Treaty of 1744.* New York: Norton, 1984.

Jennings, Gary. "An American Captivity." *American Heritage,* 19(5): 64-71, 1968.

Johnson, Patricia Givens. *Irish Burks of Colonial Virginia and New River.* Blacksburg, VA: Walpa Pub. 1992.

————. *James Patton and the Appalachian Colonists.* Verona, VA: McClure, 1973.

————. *A History of Middle New River Settlements and Contiguous Territory.* Commonwealth Press, Inc., 1969.

Kegley, Mary B. and F. B Kegley. *Early Adventurers on the Western Water.* Orange, VA: Green Publishers, 1980.

Kelle, Paul. "Historic Fort Loudoun," Vonore, TN: Fort Loudoun Association, 1958.

Kephart, Horace. *Our Southern Highlanders: A Narrative of Adventure in the Southern Appalachians and a Study of Life Among the Mountaineers.* Knoxville: Univ. of TN Press, 1976.

Kerber, Linda. *Women of the Republic: Intellect and Ideology in Revolutionary America.* Chapel Hill: Univ. of NC Press, 1980.

Kerby, Robert L. "The Other War in 1774: Dunmore's War." *West Virginia History,* 36(1): 1-16, 1974.

Kercheval, Samuel. *A History of the Valley of Virginia.* Woodstock, VA: J. Gatewood, printer, 1850.

Levy, Peter B. *100 Key Documents in American Democracy.* Westport, CN: Greenwood Press, 1994.

Lewis, Margaret. *The Common-place Book of Me: The Diary of Margaret Lynn Lewis.* Compiled by Mrs. William Roland Miller, Jr., and Mrs. James Clifton Wheat, Jr. National Society of the Colonial Dames in Virginia, 1976.

Lyman Chalkley, *Chronicles of the Scotch-Irish Settlement in Virginia, Vols. I, II, III.* Extracted from the Original Court Records of Augusta County, 1745-18, Rosslyn, VA, 1912-1913.

Mason, Augustus Luncy Mason. *Romance and Tragedy of Pioneer Life.* Cincinnati: Jones Brothers and Company, 1883.

McKnight, Charles. *Our Western Border, Its Life, Combats, Adventures, Forays, Massacres, Captivities, Scouts, Red Chiefs, Pioneer Women, One Hundred Years Ago.* Philadelphia: J. C. McCurdy & Co., 1875.

Mitchell, Robert D. *Commercialism and Frontier Perspectives on the Early Shenandoah Valley.* Charlottesville: Univ. of VA Press, 1977.

Nash, Gary B. *Red, White, and Black: The Peoples of Early America.* Englewood Cliffs, NJ: Prentice-Hall, 1982.

Nash, Roderick. *Wilderness and the American Mind.* New Haven, CN: Yale Univ. Press, 1982.

Noble, Allen G., ed. *To Build in a New Land: Ethnic Landscapes in North America.* Baltimore: Johns Hopkins Univ. Press, 1992.

Norton, Mary Beth. *Liberty's Daughters: The Revolutionary Experience of American Women, 1750-1800.* Boston: Little, Brown, 1980.

Rhys, Isaac. *The Transformation of Virginia: 1740-1790.* Chapel Hill: Univ. of NC Press, 1982.

Rice, Otis K. *History of the New River Gorge Area.* Montgomery, WV: West Virginia Institute of Technology, 1984.

Rouse, Parke. *The Great Wagon Road: From Philadelphia to the South.* New York: McGraw-Hill, 1973.

Ryan, Mary P. *Womanhood in America: From Colonial Times to the Present.* New York: New Viewpoints, 1979.

Schlissel, Lillian. *Women's Diaries of the Westward Journey.* New York: Schoken Books, 1982.

Seaver, James E. *A Narrative of the Life of Mrs. Mary Jemison.* Syracuse Univ. Press, 1990.

Smith, Abbot Emerson, *Colonists in Bondage; White Servitude and Convict Labor in America, 1607-1776.* Chapel Hill: Univ. of NC Press, 1947.

Spruill, Julia Cherry. *Women's Life and Work in the Southern Colonies.* Chapel Hill: Univ. of NC Press, 1938.

Taylor, Colin F., and William C. Sturtevant. *The Native Americans: The Indigenous People of North America.* New York: Smithmark, 1996.

The Appalachian Indian Frontier: The Edmond Atkin Report and Plan of 1755.

Thwaites, Reuben Gold, and Luise Phelps Kellogg, ed. Documentary history of Dunmore's war, 1774, from the Draper manuscripts in the library of the Wisconsin historical society and published at the charge of the Wisconsin society of the Sons of the American revolution. Madison, WI Historical Society, 1905.

Toner, J. M., ed., *Journal of My Journey Over the Mountains, 1747-1748, by George Washington.* Albany, NY: Joel Munsell's Sons, Publishers, 1892.

Trans-Allegheny Pioneers. Charleston, WV: Kanawha Valley Pub. Co., 1931.

Ulrich. *Good Wives.* New York: Oxford Univ. Press, 1970.

Washburn, Wilcomb E., ed. *The Garland Library of Narratives of North American Indian Captivities.* New York: Garland Publishing Company, 1975.

Wilson, Howard McKnight. *Great Valley Patriots: Western Virginia in the Struggle for Liberty: A Bicentennial Project Sponsored by Augusta County Historical Society, Staunton, VA.* Verona, VA: McClure Press, 1976.

Wintz, William D. *Annals of the Great Kanawha.* Charleston, WV: Pictorial Histories, 1993.

Withers, Alexander Scott. *Chronicles of Border Warfare.* Clarksburg, VA: J. Israel, 1831.

Index